The Joy of Green Cleaning

Leslie Reichert The Cleaning Coach
Teaching and encouraging others in the art of homekeeping and green cleaning, so you can enjoy a good life!

Fun, Fast, Green... and Totally Clean!

The Joy of Green Cleaning

Leslie Reichert
Certified Green Cleaner

Revised 6th Edition

The Joy of Green Cleaning

Revised 6th Edition

A handy resource book for green cleaning

Leslie Reichert

Her mission is to teach and encourage others in the art of homekeeping and green cleaning, so you can enjoy a good life!

The recipes in this book are designed as a reference. All should be tested prior to use in your home.

Internet addresses and telephone numbers given to this book were accurate at the time of printing.

Original print 2008

This book is now in its sixth printing 2015

Cover Design by Jennifer Reichert

Editing by Jodi Peterson

Photographs used with permission

Illustrations by Lindsey Reichert

Photo enhancements by Richard Ervin Photography   Harwich MA

Cl Publishing   Uxbridge, MA

All rights reserved. No part of this book may be reproduced or utilized in any form or by any means, electronic or mechanical, including photocopying and recording, or by any information storage and retrieval system, without written permission from the publisher.

 WITH MANY THANKS

This book is dedicated to my family, who are my raving fans! - Especially my husband, Austin, who inspired me to "get back in there and make something happen!" Thank you for your love and support.

And to the women in my life that have encouraged me along the way -Mom, Trudy-mom, Jen, Lindsey and all my friends that have worked by me and with me.

A special thank-you to Ann! I still feel your two hands pushing me to do it! Thank-you.

Leslie, the cleaning coach

...encourage the young women to love their husbands, to love their children, to be sensible, pure, keepers of the home... so that the word of God will not be dishonored

Titus 3-5

Items in this book can be found at Leslie's online store, ShopGreenCleaning.com. It has been in existence for over 20 years and provides the best in cleaning products

ShopGreenCleaning.com

508-234-4626

facebook.com/shopgreencleaning

Part of the proceeds of this book will be donated to Peace of Bread Community Kitchen in Whitinsville, MA

Copyright by Leslie Reichert 2008/2011/2015

Do you have a great green recipe…

tip, idea or just a memory you would like to see featured in our next book? Visit our web site at thecleaningcoach.us and email us to submit your favorite green cleaning recipe or tip. Or you can e-mail them to us at:

Leslie, The Cleaning Coach

cleaningcoach@yahoo.com

Don't forget to include your name, street address, phone number and e-mail address. If we select your entry, your name will appear with your submission… and you will receive a FREE copy of the book!

Contents

Daily Kitchen Cleaners 10

Metal Cleaners 28

Bathroom Cleaners 35

Floor Cleaners 57

Furniture Care 62

Laundry Care 67

Nursery Care........................73

Other Green Ideas 79

Resources & Information 92

What is the big deal about greening your cleaning?

Did you know that my great-grandmother cleaned her home with four simple things: white vinegar, salt, baking soda and Borax. My great-grandmother lived to be very old and she cleaned her whole life without using antibacterial spray, bleach, or the other things we are told we need to use to keep our homes truly clean.

The truth is that most regular cleaning can be done without any toxic chemicals. Simple things in your panty can do a great job cleaning your home. Baking soda, vinegar, sea salt, lemon juice, and hydrogen peroxide can be used in place of most grocery store cleaners. And if you don't want to mix up your own homemade cleaners there are green companies creating cleaning products that are made with simple ingredients-and they really work.

One of the questions I receive every day is "How do I disinfect my home?" Honestly, I doubt that we need to do this at all. What we have done recently is try to kill <u>all</u> the bacteria in our homes. Some people don't realize that there are good bacteria and bad bacteria, and the only thing that lives through a cleaning with antibacterial products are the bad bacteria. These bacteria survive and create an even stronger form that is resistant to the antibacterial agents you use to kill them. So if you think about it, you may be doing more damage to your body by using chemicals than the "bad" bacteria can possibly do to you.

This book contains recipes for cleaners you can use every day in your kitchen, your bathroom, on your floors, in your laundry, and with your furniture using simple products you keep in your pantry. Some of the ingredients, like soap flakes, are rarely produced but I have found suppliers for all of them and have them listed in the back of the book. (We also have references to products that you can try if you don't want to make your own.)

I have also been privileged to be introduced to the researchers at the University of MA, Lowell who are working on performance tests for the recipes in this book using the Green Seal methods know in the industry as GS37. The TURI laboratory specializes in offering alternatives to hazardous cleaning products that exist for nearly every type of household cleaner. I am looking forward to working closely with them to also learn how new technologies can change the way we clean. You can see more about the TURI Labs at www.turi.org

So go ahead and give these recipes a try! I always love to see the faces of people when I show them what a cut lemon and some salt can really do. You'll be surprised too! And I want to hear about your successes! In this book you will see stories from people just like you who may have been skeptical, but have found that these recipes really do work. Make sure you share your stories with me and your friends. Together we can change the world, one spray bottle at a time!

If you would like more information about green cleaning or would like to see some of my "how to" videos, just go to www.greencleaningcoach.com You can also friend me on facebook at www.facebook.com/LeslieReichert

Happy Cleaning!

Leslie

Leslie Reichert

The Cleaning Coach

www.greencleaningcoach.com

mailto:cleaningcoach@yahoo.com

Some General Tips

- Borax will dissolve better in hot water than in cold. Try this if you are finding your spray bottles getting clogged with your cleaner.
- Do not mix bleach or ammonia with any of these cleaners.
- Soap Flakes tend to work better in hot water, but if you dissolve them first in hot water, you can add them to a cold water wash without any problems.

Daily Kitchen Cleaners

Multi-purpose Cleaner

1 teaspoon borax

½ teaspoon washing soda

2 tablespoon vinegar

½ teaspoon liquid castile soap*

2 cups very hot water

Warm up the water in the microwave for 45 seconds. Add each of the ingredients in small amounts into the hot water. Mix while adding these ingredients. Add the soap last and don't mix it a lot (you don't want a lot of foam.) Rinse thoroughly.

Tools to use: Microfiber cloths, microfiber mop or sparkle sponges*

Non-toxic alternatives: Mrs. Meyers* all-purpose cleaner in different scents, Caldrea* all-purpose cleaner or Bi-o-Kleen* all-purpose cleaner.

Modern Mermaids Everyday Cleaner

Disinfecting Spray Cleaner

8 ounces of white vinegar

4 ounces vodka or rubbing alcohol

4 ounces of hydrogen peroxide

6 drops tea tree oil for disinfecting

6 drops of any other essential oil for scent

Mix the essential oils to the white vinegar in a spray bottle. Add the alcohol and hydrogen peroxide. Shake together and use to clean and disinfect in the kitchen or bathroom. The hydrogen peroxide will break down into water when it's exposed to light. Just top of the container with more hydrogen peroxide right before you are ready to use it again.

This mixture can be used on countertops and floors. It is good cleaning and disinfecting. Avoid using it on sealed countertops as the acid from the vinegar can break down the coating.

1/3 c grain alcohol
1/3 c cleaning vinegar
1/3 c hydrogen peroxide

Tea Tree Oil disinfects.

All-Purpose Liquid Cleaner

16 ounces of club soda

1 tablespoon baking soda

4 drops dish soap

6 drops any essential oil for fragrance

Mix the dish soap and baking soda together, and then add to the club soda. Add your choice of essential oil. Place into a spray bottle.

This mixture can be used on countertops and floors. It is good for all around cleaning.

To make a heavy duty cleaner, add 3 tablespoons of borax.

Better Life - Whatever All Purpose Cleaner

Daily Counter Cleanser

1 cup white vinegar

1 cup water

8 drops essential oil in lemon scent

Mix the vinegar and water together. Add the oil for a fresh scent. To make the mixture stronger, heat it in the microwave. Use the mixture in a spray bottle. Avoid using on sealed granite, marble or other sealed stone countertops.

Tools: Microfiber cloths

Heinz Distilled White Vinegar

Daily Dish Soap

> "I enjoyed your style and information. I have cleaned all the windows in my house with your 'blue cloth' and love the results! Quick and thorough."
>
> Paula F.
>
> South Weymouth, MA

3 cups castile soap*

16 drops essential oil

Mix the soap with the oil of your choice for a fragrance to fill the kitchen every time you wash a dish. If you have a dispenser that will turn the soap to foam, add 3 cups of water. This can be used for dishes or for hand soap.

Casabella Dispensing Brush

Baking Soda Scrubbing Paste

2 tablespoons baking soda

6 drops dish soap

Water to make paste

Mix the baking soda with the dish soap in small amounts. Add the water to make a thin paste.

Use this paste for difficult areas during cleaning. You can use this to scrub out stainless steel sinks as well as counters and other difficult areas.

Tools: Scrubby sponges, sparkle sponges*, skoy clothes.

Mrs. Meyer's Surface Scrub

Green Gentle Scrub

This mixture is a great alternative to a commercial "scrub". (Try to avoid using chlorine bleach for cleaning.)

1 cup borax

½ cup salt

Olive oil or dish soap to create paste

6 drops essential oils for fragrance

Create a paste that will act like a liquid scrub for cleaning stains from countertops and in your sink. Rinse thoroughly.

Tools: scrubby sponges, sparkle sponges* fine grade steel wool.

Casabella Sparkle Sponges

Green Powder Scrub

This mixture can be kept in a shaker container by the sink and will act just like any "over the counter" powder cleanser.

1 cup borax

2 cups salt (sea salt for more aggressive cleanser)

2 cups baking soda

8 drops essential oils for fragrance

Mix borax, salt and baking soda thoroughly. After they are completely mixed together, add the essential oils for fragrance.

Keep this mixture in a shaker container with a lid. Use it for cleaning stains on counters and sinks. Rinse thoroughly.

Tools: Skoy cloths* and sponges

"I tried this Green Cleaning Soft Scrub. At first, I was hesitant of my new discovery, but it worked just as well as our regular cleaner. I was speechless as I scrubbed the sink and spots, stains and other messes just seemed to come off at the glide of the sponge. I have adopted this soft scrub into our home. I love it!!"

Stephanie B.

"I washed my kitchen sink with your Green Cleaning Scrub. You were right – it does clean as well as Comet!"

Mary H.

Framingham, MA

Foaming Sink Cleanser

½ cup baking soda

1 tablespoon cream of tartar

¼ cup vinegar

Mix baking soda and cream of tartar together. Sprinkle them into the sink, lightly covering the bottom. Put vinegar in a spray bottle and spray the entire sink. The mixture will start to foam. Scrub the foam with a scrubby sponge. Rinse completely to remove any leftover film from the baking soda.

Oven Cleaner

1 cup baking soda

2 cups white vinegar in a spray bottle

Sprinkle the base of the oven with the baking soda. Spray the vinegar over the baking soda to make a light foam. Let the foam sit as long as you can. Keep spraying the baking soda to keep it moist. For the side of the oven, mix some baking soda with water to make a thick paste and spread it on the sides of the oven. Spray the paste with vinegar and leave it sit as long as you can. Wipe off the excess paste and then rinse with hot water.

**Note: If you have a self-cleaning stove you need to check with the manufacturer to make sure you can use this recipe. Self-cleaning ovens have a special coating on the inside and certain elements can damage the coating and ruin the self-cleaning feature. We don't want that!

Coffeemaker Cleaner

2 cups white vinegar

Run completely through the coffee pot maker. Rinse by running an entire pot of water through the machine.

Paste for cleaning the coffee pot

¼ cup baking soda

3 tablespoons sea salt

1 teaspoon lemon juice

Mix these ingredients to make paste. Rub the inside of the pot with the paste and a skoy cloth*. Rinse thoroughly.

Tip: To clean the inside of a coffee thermos place 3-5 ice cubes inside and sprinkle with salt. Swish and rinse.

Cutting Board Sanitizer

Wood Boards

1 lemon/ lime / grapefruit

Small dish of salt

Cut the fruit in half and dip it into salt. Using the salt as a scrub, lightly rub the fruit over the cutting board. Squeeze the fruit as you are rubbing to get the juice to flow. Rinse completely when done.

Plastic or Glass Boards

¼ cup lemon juice

2 cups water

Let soak for 15 minutes and rinse completely.

Dishwasher Powder

¼ cup citric acid (Tang drink mix) or 1 package of Kool-Aid non-sweetened lemonade

1½ cup borax

5 drops castile soap

15 drops essential oil for fragrance

Mix the powders, soap and oil and stir. Keep in an airtight container. Use up to ¼ cup per load of dishes depending on how dirty they are. Always make sure to rinse the dishes if you don't intent to run the washer right away. This keeps the dishwasher smelling fresh and you won't need a lot of dishwashing powder.

.

Stainless Steel – Chrome Polish

"I just wanted to let you know that I mixed up a batch of your stainless steel/chrome polish.

I used it to clean the stainless steel back splash on my Viking stove. It was fantastic! My stove has not been this clean since it was new. Much better than the commercial stainless steel cleaners, and without the odor. It even removed some of the burnt on residue that would never come off before. I can't wait to try some of your other recipes. Thank you"
Jen S

1 cup baking soda

¼ cup lemon juice

3 tablespoons borax

Club soda to make paste

Mix baking soda, borax and lemon juice together. Add enough club soda to make paste. Apply the paste to the metal you are cleaning with a soft cloth or skoy cloth*. Rinse with plain club soda. Finish by polishing with a clean cloth.

Tools: Skoy cloth or paper towel to apply paste. Wipe with cotton rags or microfiber cloth.

Skoy Cloths

Dishwasher Rinse Aid

½ cup lemon juice

½ cup club soda

2 tablespoons borax

Warm the club soda in the microwave for 30 seconds. Dissolve borax in the club soda, and then add lemon juice. Put into a container with a tapered spout and pour it into the rinse aid dispenser of your dishwasher.

Illustration by Lindsey Reichert

Orange/Lemon Infused White Vinegar

Peel from one fresh orange or lemon

1 16 ounce bottle of distilled white vinegar

Airtight container

Place the peel of the orange or lemon into the distilled white vinegar. Cover and let stand for two weeks. Remove the peels and place the vinegar in a spray bottle. Add some distilled water or vodka and you have a great all purpose cleaner.

Infusing the white vinegar with the peels of an orange or lemon combines the acidic power of the vinegar with the acidic properties of the orange/lemon. It also creates in nicely scented cleaner that is extremely powerful.

Metal Cleaners

Copper Cleaner

¼ cup concentrated lemon juice

¼ cup table or sea salt

Warm the lemon juice in the microwave for 30 seconds. Then add the salt to make a thick paste. Apply to the copper with a microfiber cloth or sponge. Wash with warm water and gentle dish soap. Dry thoroughly with a soft cloth.

An alternative

¼ cup ketchup

3 tablespoons cream of tartar

Mix ingredients together and rub onto copper. Let sit for 3 to 5 minutes and rinse with warm water. Wash the copper with gentle dish soap and dry with a soft cloth.

Silver Tarnish Remover

Soak the silver to be cleaned in warm water and 2 cups of salt. Then, using a soft cloth, rub the silver with toothpaste. Use a toothbrush to get into tight areas that need cleaning. Rinse in the sink filled with warm water and 3 teaspoons of baking soda. Use a clean soft cloth to dry.

Cape Cod Silver Polish

Silver:
Toothpaste
or
heavy duty tinfoil - add vinegar - add silver - If it doesn't come clean scrub w/ toothpaste

Stainless Steel – Chrome

¼ cup baking soda

¼ cup borax

Lemon juice to make paste

Mix the dry ingredients together. Add enough lemon juice to make a thin paste. Apply to the metal with a sponge or skoy* cloth in a circular motion. Rinse with warm water and a gentle dish soap.

Rust Remover

1 full can of original Coke

This is an amazing solution to removing rust from everything from kitchen utensils to gardening tools. Let the item soak in the can of Coke overnight and it will come out shiny and new.

This will also work for removing rust stains from fixtures in your bathroom. Let it sit overnight in the toilet and you will be rust free!

"This book is great if you want to get away from harsh chemicals and nasty side-effects, while still getting your home and belongings squeaky clean."

The Daily Grommet

www.dailygrommet.com

Chrome – Copper – Brass

1 whole lemon

1 small dish of sea or regular salt

Cut the lemon in half and dip in the salt. Rub the salt onto the tarnished metal. Squeeze the juice of the lemon out slowly to cover the metal. Once clean, wash in warm water and a gentle dish soap.

"I received the Joy of Green Cleaning book and accessories as a Christmas gift and it was by far the best one! I wanted to tell you how much I love the book and every suggestion in it. I loved it so much that I wanted to ask your permission to share it on my blog, everydayorigionals."

Lindsey T.
everydayorigionals

Pewter Cleaner

½ cup flour

1 cup white vinegar

1 teaspoon table salt

Combine all these ingredients into a thick paste. Rub onto the pewter item in a circle. Wipe off thoroughly and then rinse the item with warm water. Dry with a soft cloth and buff.

Bathroom Cleaners

Daily Anti-bacterial Spray

1 cup white vinegar

1 cup club soda

¼ cup hydrogen peroxide

8 drops Tea Tree oil for disinfectant

Mix liquid and put into spray bottle. Add oil for disinfecting properties. Use a dark bottle and store in a dark area. You can add more hydrogen peroxide before using this spray. The peroxide will break down in light.

Tools: Use microfiber cloths to pick up bacteria. Wash them in hot water, whether in the dishwasher or laundry after cleaning to remove bacteria and dirt. If they are high quality microfiber cloths, you can place them in the microwave wet for 2-3 minutes to disinfect.

"For Christmas gifts I gave spray bottles with microfiber cloths and recipes for green cleaning, My sisters and friends wanted to know more and had great results when using them. Yippee. Spread the word this stuff works. And my hands feel better."

Lynn M.

Attleboro, MA

Soft Cleansing Scrub

½ cup baking soda

¼ cup borax

¼ cup washing soda

¼ cup salt (table or coarse)

¼ cup oxygen bleach – powder

1 teaspoon cream of tartar

3 drops castile soap or dish detergent

¼ cup vinegar

½ cup vodka

8 drops essential oil for scent

Mix together all dry ingredients. Add the drops of castile soap into the dry ingredients until mixed thoroughly. Heat the white vinegar in microwave until very hot. Then mix into the dry ingredients. The vinegar will foam but will be fine to mix into the dry ingredients. Add the vodka and stir until completely mixed together. It will seem very wet, but let it sit and mix again. If it continues to feel too wet add some additional baking soda. Place in a jar with lid and use with a sponge to clean sinks, tubs and countertops. This mixture is also great for glass topped stoves.

Concentrated All Purpose Cleaner

3 drops castile soap

¼ cup washing soda

1 cup white vinegar heated to boiling in microwave

¼ cup vodka

8 drops essential oil for scent

4 drops Tea Tree oil

Microwave vinegar in the microwave until it's boiling. Add the washing soda and stir until it is totally dissolved. Add the three drops of castile soap and all the essential oil. Then add vodka and shake. Place the mixture in a container for storage. When ready to use mix with water at a ratio of 1:4. You can use this mixture on counters, sinks and more.

Anti-bacterial Cleaner

1 tablespoon soap flakes*

¾ cup hot water

¼ teaspoon baking soda or soda crystals*

¼ teaspoon Tea Tree oil

2 tablespoons isopropyl alcohol (rubbing)

Dissolve the soap flakes in the hot water heated in the microwave for one minute. Slowly add all the other ingredients to the liquid mixture. Place the cleaner in a spray bottle.

Use this mixture to disinfect areas around the toilet and the toilet itself. Use a microfiber cloth to clean the area completely.

Soap Flakes

Bathroom Powder Scrub

1 cup borax

1 cup baking soda

½ cup sea salt

6 drops essential oils for fragrance

Mix all the dry ingredients. Add the essential oils for fragrance. Keep in a shaker container for cleaning the bathroom sink and tub. Do not use this mixture on fiberglass tubs. The salt could scratch. Just mix up the recipe without salt for fiberglass.

Tools: Scrubby sponge, skoy* cloths, sparkle sponge* or sponge.

Tip: Make sure to disinfect your skoy cloths* and sponges in the wash or the microwave for 2 -3 minutes (wet) after using on bathroom fixtures.

Gentle Scrub

¾ cup baking soda or soda crystals*

¼ cup powdered milk

1/8 cup liquid castile soap*

6 drops essential oil for scent

Enough water to make paste

This mixture is great for gently scrubbing extremely sensitive fixtures in your bathroom. Just use the paste with a soft cotton or microfiber cloth.

Tub and Tile Scrub

1 cup borax

½ cup sea salt

½ cup baking soda or soda crystals*

¼ cup olive oil

5 drops dish soap

Club soda

Mix borax, salt and baking soda completely. Add olive oil and dish soap to make a paste. Add club soda until you have a creamy paste. Keep in a container with a screw top lid. This mixture should not be used on surfaces that might scratch. You can leave out the sea salt for fiberglass tubs.

Tools: Scrubby sponge, sparkle sponge*.

Tip: Apply the paste in circular motion and if the tile is stained, leave the paste on for two hours. Then spray the paste with white vinegar to form a foamy rinse. Wipe away the foam with warm water and rinse thoroughly.

Tile Cleaner

1 cup vinegar or hydrogen peroxide

¼ cup borax

1 gallon hot water

Heat the vinegar in the microwave until boiling. Dissolve the borax into the vinegar. Mix the entire solution into a gallon bucket of hot water. Use a stiff brush to wash wall and floor tiles.

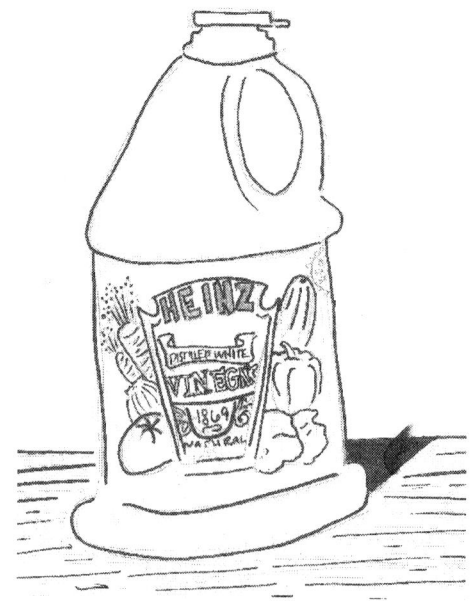

Illustration by Lindsey Reichert

Citrus Tub Scrubber

Great for porcelain tubs

¼ cup baking soda

¼ cup castile soap*

2 vitamin C tablets

Crush the vitamin C tablets until a smooth powder. Add the powder to the castile soap. Then add enough baking soda until you get a smooth paste. Use on a scrubby sponge or skoy* cloth to apply directly to the tub. Apply in a circular motion and leave for a few minutes. Rinse with warm water

"Having a son that was in the NICU for 11 days after he was born, I know all too well how careful we are as parents to keep our homes germ free but at the same time, it seems like a rather risky trade off when we're using chemicals that can do more harm than good. For those not quite ready to make the jump to cleaning exclusively, Leslie's book does offer some green commercial brand alternatives which I like."

Chic Simple Moms

chicsimplemoms.com

Whitening – Scouring Powder

1 cup baking soda

2 tablespoons cream of tarter

1/8 cup of borax

6 drops of lemon juice or lemon essential oil

Mix all the dry ingredients. Add the oil or juice and place in a shaker container. Use with an abrasive scrubbing sponge or very fine steel wool.

Tip: Mix with a small amount of hydrogen peroxide to make a paste and let it sit for up to an hour. Scrub in a circular motion and wipe clean.

Toilet Bowl Powder

1 cup borax

1 cup baking soda or soda crystals*

1 cup salt

6 drops Tea Tree oil for disinfecting

Mix all the dry ingredients. Add the tea tree oil to make powder a disinfecting powder. Sprinkle the powder in the toilet as needed and scrub with a clean toilet brush. For added cleansing add a cup of white vinegar to the toilet after scrubbing with the powder. Flush.

Tip: Turn off the water to the toilet and flush so all the water empties out of the base. Sprinkle the cleansing powder directly to the porcelain and scrub directly with a scrubby sponge. Add the vinegar and let sit for 1-2 hours then turn on the water and flush. Now you have one clean toilet!

Toilet / Porcelain Cleaner

2 cups water

¼ cup castile soap* or dish soap

1 teaspoon Tea Tree oil

Mix together and use sparingly in the toilet. To scrub off stains and rings from hard water, use a handled pumice stone*. Also drain the toilet of the water by turning off the supply line and flushing. This will not dilute the cleaner.

¼ cup vinegar

½ cup borax

3 tablespoons lemon juice or hydrogen peroxide

Heat the vinegar and lemon juice in the microwave for 30 seconds. Mix in the borax until it turns into a paste. Use a stiff brush to apply directly to the mold. Let the mixture set to let the acid in the vinegar and lemon juice kill the mold. Then finish scrubbing the area and rinse with warm water.

Illustration by Lindsey Reichert

Mold Spray

1 teaspoon borax

3 tablespoons vinegar

½ cup hot water

Heat the water in the microwave for 30 seconds. Dissolve the borax in the water, and then add the vinegar. Reheat the entire mixture and put in a spray bottle. Spray directly on the mold and let sit. Wipe the area with a scrubby sponge and then rinse with water and a microfiber cloth.

"I went back to using Borax and vinegar for household cleaning. For some time now I've wanted to move away from things that harm me, my family, and the environment. Thanks for reminding me it's not good to be using all these germ killers... we need some germs in our life so our bodies can learn how to fight them. I hadn't thought about that until you mentioned it. I've since heard doctors say the same thing...send the kids out to play and let them get dirty...that's how our bodies learn to fight germs. That's when I realized I want a clean home, but not a sterile home."

Diane
PBS

Foamy Drain Cleaner

1 cup white vinegar

3 tablespoons baking soda

Heat the vinegar in microwave for 1 minute. Pour the baking soda down the drain, followed by the hot vinegar. Let it sit for 10 to 15 minutes. While waiting, heat a pot of hot water and pour down the drain to remove buildup in pipes. Repeat as needed.

Tip: Find a small bottle brush and go down the drain with the brush. You can also try a plunger to remove more of the buildup.

Grout Cleaner

1 cup Oxygen Bleach*

Hot white vinegar to make paste

Mix the oxygen bleach powder with hot vinegar to create thick paste. Using a toothbrush or stiff grout brush, apply the paste to the grout. Let it sit for 1-2 hours. Rinse and repeat if necessary.

Tools: Use a stiff toothbrush, grout brush or gentle wire brush to apply paste. Wash off with a cotton rag or microfiber cloth.

Hair Spray Remover

½ cup fabric softener

½ cup hot water

Mix the two ingredients and put into a spray bottle. Spray directly on hairspray build-up. Let the mixture sit for a few minutes. Wipe with a scrubby sponge.

Tools: Scrubby sponge, sparkle sponge or skoy cloth*.

Sparkle sponges are safe for fiberglass

Glass and Mirror Cleaners

2 tablespoons white vinegar

½ cup cornstarch

2 liter bottle club soda

Mix club soda with cornstarch until dissolved. Add the white vinegar and put into spray bottle. Spray directly to mirrors and inside of windows.

****

1 cup alcohol in spray bottle

Spray directly to mirrors

****

1 teaspoon dish soap

½ cup white vinegar

3 cups distilled water

Place all ingredients in spray bottle. Spray directly onto windows and mirrors.

****

For streak free glass, use a high grade microfiber cloth* with very hot water. It will leave your glass without streaks, lint free and will repel dust for days!

"I went to your demonstration at my local school a few weeks ago and started trying your products which I made that night. They are amazing and smell great! Most importantly, the cloth is wonderful. Thanks again."

Annemarie K.

Window Cleaner

To remove Acid Rain spots:

½ cup vinegar

½ cup lemon juice

Mix together and apply to window with a scrubby sponge or sparkle sponge.

Microfiber Blue Cloth

Linen Spray for Bathroom Towels

1 cup vodka

1 cup distilled water

16 drops of lavender essential oil

Mix the ingredients and put into a spray bottle. Spray directly onto towels, sheets and pillows. Lavender oil has relaxation properties that will give your bedroom and bathroom a lovely relaxing scent.

Bathroom Floor Cleaner

¼ cup lemon juice

8 drops dish soap

3 tablespoons skim milk or dry powdered milk

Mix the ingredients with 16 ounces of warm water and put into a spray bottle. Spray directly onto floor and use a wet cloth or wet microfiber cloth to clean the floor. Rinse if needed.

"Leslie has mastered what many of us know but few practice: the art of cleaning naturally, without relying solely on store-bought products, harnessing the power of nature instead."

Sara Snow

Author of "Sara Snow's Fresh Living"

Daily Shower Cleaner

1 cup white vinegar

8 drops tea tree oil

6 drops essential oil for scent

Mix the ingredients and put into a spray bottle. Spray directly onto your shower stall daily. This mixture will keep soap scum and mold to a minimum. It is also good for fighting mold and mildew on your shower curtain. You can also wash your shower curtain with this mixture in your washing machine. Just place the curtain in the washer with some towels and they will work on removing the soap scum along with the daily cleaner. Place the curtain in the dryer for just a few minutes to make it warm and easy to hang.

Floor Cleaners

No Wax Floor Cleaner

¼ cup lemon juice

8 drops dish soap

3 tablespoons skim milk or dry powdered milk

Mix the ingredients with 16 ounces of warm water and put into a spray bottle. Spray directly onto floor using a wet cloth or wet microfiber cloth to clean the floor. Rinse if needed. This method does not need a bucket. You will use less cleaner and less water.

"I love this book! A simple yet necessary resource for learning how to take the toxins out of your home. She is helping families – and the world – with one book"

Ed Begley Jr.

Environmental Leader, author and actor

"The Joy of Green Cleaning by Leslie Reichert delivers on its promise to help consumers find deep satisfaction in making effective green cleaning products from items in their pantry. The tested and proven range of recipes enables readers to clean up almost all their cleaning processes easily and at low cost."

Allen Rathey, President, The Healthy House Institute (HHI)

Grout Cleaner

1 cup Oxygen Bleach*

Hot white vinegar to make paste

Mix the oxygen bleach powder with hot vinegar to create thick paste. Using a toothbrush or stiff grout brush, apply the paste to the grout. Let it sit for 1-2 hours. Rinse and repeat if necessary.

Tools: Use a stiff toothbrush, grout brush or gentle wire brush to apply paste. Wash off with a cotton rag or microfiber cloth.

Hardwood Floor Cleaner

1 teaspoon dish soap

1/8 cup white vinegar

32 ounces hot water

Mix all ingredients and place in a spray bottle. Use a dry microfiber mop after vacuuming the hardwood floor. Spray the floor with cleaner and wipe with the dry microfiber mop. This mixture will leave the floor, clean without a waxy buildup.

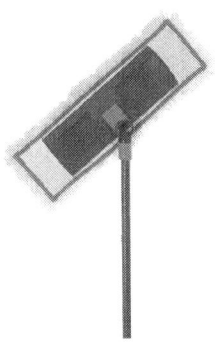

Tile Floor Cleaner

1 cup white vinegar

¼ cup borax

Bucket of hot water

Pour the vinegar into bucket of hot water then add borax. Use microfiber or sponge mop to clean tile floor.

Tip: The best way to clean floors is on your hands and knees. The next best way is with a microfiber mop. It will make it look like you cleaned it by hand.

Furniture Care

Lemony Furniture Re-newer

> "My 20 year old daughter has decided this is the best furniture polish on the planet. She wants to bottle it and create her own business selling this product. Too bad it's so simple – anyone can make it!"
>
> Jennifer R.

This mixture is great for old or dried wood furniture. It will also bring back a glow to dark woods.

3 tablespoons lemon juice concentrate

3 tablespoons olive oil

Mix together thoroughly and put on a clean cloth. Wipe the piece of furniture with the grain of the wood. Let the mixture sit for 15 minutes, then wipe the excess off with a clean cotton cloth. (cotton baby diapers – unfolded - are perfect for your furniture.)

Lemon Furniture Polish

¼ cup olive oil

¼ cup white vinegar

¼ c lemon juice concentrate

Mix the lemon juice and vinegar together first, and then add olive oil. Place mixture on clean cloth and rub into the wood, going with the grain. Let it sit for a few minutes. The furniture will look very dull and smeary. Buff with a clean soft cloth and watch your furniture shine. Wipe off excess oil.

Light Dusting Spray

This mixture can be used to just lightly dust furniture. It is great for removing pollen.

2 regular tea bags

1 tablespoon lemon juice

3 cups water

Place the 3 cups of water in the microwave for 2 minutes or until boiling. Put both tea bags into the hot water for 2 minutes. While leaving the tea bags in the water, pour yourself one cup of tea, and go relax for a while. Leave the tea bags in the water until the entire mixture has cooled completely. Squeeze out tea bags and place cooled tea in spray bottle. Using a soft cloth, spray the mixture onto the cloth and dust.

"I tried my green cloth - it works great! What a great dust cloth! I'm impressed. I will definitely tell others about your products. I have a website: delightfullywed.com I'm going to share your products and book on that blog - new brides would definitely benefit from using your products."

Debbie

Delightfullywed.com

Awesome Furniture Restorer

This recipe is great for dried wood on furniture or just to give it a new luster. It will clean the wood as well as polish. You need to leave some time to do this procedure, as it is a polish and not just for dusting. I would recommend doing this every six months to keep your furniture in its best condition.

¼ cup mayonnaise (regular, not fat free)

¼ cup olive oil

3 tablespoons lemon juice

Mix the mayonnaise and olive oil in a small bowl. Add the lemon juice. Apply the mixture with a small sponge or skoy* cloth. Let it sit for a few minutes. Wipe off excess with a clean soft cloth.

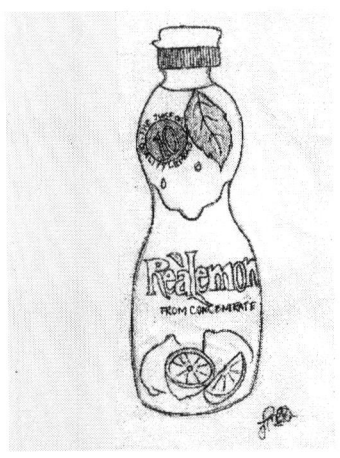

Illustration by Lindsey Reichert

Laundry Care

Great-grandma's Laundry Soap

2 cups soap flakes*

1 cup baking soda or soda crystals*

1 cup borax

1 cup washing soda

Mix all the ingredients thoroughly, and then place in plastic or glass container with a lid. This soap works best with hot water.

For top loading washing machines- use ½ to 1 cup, 2 cups for very heavily soiled clothing.

For front loading and HE machines, use 2 tablespoons.

* freeze Ivory soap bars/grate then Add 20-30 drops of essential oil

Use wool dryer balls in place of dryer sheets

Liquid Laundry Soap

1 cup soap flakes*

¼ cup baking soda or soda crystals*

½ cup borax

2 tablespoons glycerin

2 cups water

Mix all the dry ingredients thoroughly. Heat the water in the microwave until boiling (2 minutes), and then mix in dry ingredients. Store the liquid in a plastic airtight container like a milk carton.

Original Soap Flakes

Fabric Softener

3 cups white vinegar

½ cup water

½ cup baking soda

8 drops of your favorite essential oil

Mix the water and the vinegar, and then heat in the microwave for 60 seconds. Dissolve the baking soda into the mixture. Add your choice of essential oils. Use in your wash, just like any store bought liquid fabric softener.

Alternatives

Add ½ cup of white vinegar, baking soda or borax to the rinse cycle to soften the water and reduce static cling.

Tip: Test your dryer filter for an invisible build-up by running it under water. If it holds water, place it in the dishwasher to remove the build up and then try to switch to a fabric softener that has less wax and oil. This will protect your dryer from over-heating as well as protect your home from an accidental dryer fire.

Laundry Bleach

¼ cup borax

¼ cup vinegar

¼ cup hydrogen peroxide

Heat the vinegar in the microwave for 30 seconds. Dissolve the borax into the vinegar, and then add the peroxide right before adding to the wash. The peroxide will not stay **active** for very long so you add it to the mixture right before using it.

Charlie's Soap All Natural Laundry Soap

Old Fashioned Laundry Whitener

Winter

This is an old remedy that will remove spots from your clothing when all else fails. Wet the clothing that has the spots with water and place it outside in the snow on a sunny day.

Summer

Wet the clothing with water and ½ cup lemon juice. Place outside in the sun and the combination of the lemon juice and sunshine will bleach the clothing a bright white.

Club Soda – cloth stains
Hydrogen Peroxide – blood, wine

Nursery Care

High Chair Cleaner

1 cup distilled white vinegar

1 cup distilled water

¼ cup hydrogen peroxide

6 drops tea tree oil

6 drops essential oil for scent

Use a microfiber cloth with this highchair cleaner. The vinegar is a natural way to kill bacteria and germs. If you don't like the smell of vinegar, you can add an essential oil to it and the oil will cancel out the vinegar smell. Now you have a great anti-bacterial spray that won't hurt the baby

Baby Toy Cleaner

1 cup hydrogen peroxide

1 cup white distilled vinegar

8 drops tea tree oil

Place in a spray bottle and also a squirt bottle and use to wash toys in the sink. Make sure you rinse them well.

Using hydrogen peroxide is a great way to clean your baby toys without using bleach. Whether you are cleaning hard plastic toys or stuffed animals the hydrogen peroxide will kill the germs. Hydrogen peroxide is used in hospitals to kill germs and is also used by dentists to whiten our teeth.

Anti-Bacterial Cleaner for the Changing Table

1 cup hydrogen peroxide

1 cup white distilled vinegar

¼ cup water

2 tablespoons borax

8 drops tea tree oil

Heat the water in the microwave for 30-60 seconds. Add the borax to the water and stir until it is completely dissolved. Place this mixture in a spray bottle and add the hydrogen peroxide and vinegar. Top with the 8 drops of tea tree oil.

Tip: Store this mixture in a dark area as the hydrogen peroxide will break down when it's exposed to light. You can add more peroxide as you use the mixture to keep it effective.

Baby Tub Cleaner

1 cup hydrogen peroxide

1 cup white distilled vinegar

1 cup bottle of club soda

8 drops tea tree oil

1 microfiber cloth

The baby tub needs to be cleaned before and after use. Spray it down with this tub spray and wipe it with a microfiber cloth. The microfiber will catch and hold the dirt and wipe it off the tub. You want to make sure you clean the tub after the bath too - you just never know what may have gotten into the water during the bath. Babies don't know how to control their bowels or bladder, so you need to use the antibacterial spray on the tub after the bath too.

Stroller Cleaner and Wipes

1 cup hydrogen peroxide

1 cup white distilled vinegar

½ cup lemon juice

8 drops tea tree oil

1 microfiber cloth

Paper towels

Plastic zip lock baggie

Keep a microfiber cloth and a small spray bottle of this stroller cleaner in the bottom of the stroller. Cleaning right when the spill or accident happens is much easier than waiting until you get home. A simple spill will harden in the hot car, and will be 10x harder to remove.

You can make a spot wipe with these same ingredients. Just soak paper towels in the mixture and store in a zip lock bag. Now you have a cleaner ready when you need it.

Other Green Ideas

Hardwood — microfiber, warm water (sm. amt. vinegar)

Horizontal Blind Cleaner

1 small bottle of club soda

1 microfiber cloth or glove

Find a spray bottle and place the club soda into the spray bottle. Spray a microfiber cloth with the club soda and wipe gently over the blinds. This mixture is for removing a light film of dust, not a heavy build up.

Casabella Microfiber Glove

Green Shoe Polish

To add a nice shine to shoes use the inside of a banana peel and wipe over the shoe. Polish with a thick microfiber cloth.

Microfiber Cleaning Cloth

Sheepskin Cleaner

½ cup castile soap or soap flakes

½ cup warm water

Combine water and soap and place in a spray bottle. If you are using soap flakes dissolve them in ½ cup of hot water and then let the soap mixture cool down. Place a light mist of the soap mixture on your sheepskin or spray a soft cloth with the mixture and apply lightly to the sheepskin with soft cloth. Rub gently and then rinse with a clean sponge dampened with cool water. Let the item air dry. Do not use heat or place the sheepskin in sunlight. Do not use any soap that contains enzymes or bleach. For cleaning large sheepskin rugs and car seat covers you can hand wash in cool water with a small amount of soap and let them air dry. It is recommended that you reshape after washing as they can become distorted.

Use baking powder combined with a few drops of your favorite essential oil to remove odors from sheepskin. Shake a small amount of the powder into wool and leave overnight. Shake out in the morning.

"Ugg" Boot Deodorizer

1 cup baking soda

1 cup corn starch

10 drops of your favorite essential oil

Mix the powder and then add the essential oil. Place the powder in a shaker container. Shake a small amount in your boots as needed. Leave the powder in the boots over night and remove in the morning before wearing. This combination will absorb moisture and remove smells, leaving your boots fresh for your next wearing.

Leather Conditioner

½ cup olive oil

¼ cup plain brewed tea

¼ cup white vinegar

Combine all three ingredients and place into a spray bottle. Shake well and spray a soft cloth or microfiber cloth with the mixture. Apply lightly to the leather. Let sit for 5 minutes and wipe up any extra.

Seige Leather Cleaner

Green Carpet Freshener

½ cup baking soda

½ cup borax

10 drops essential oil in lemon

Mix the dry ingredients and then add the essential oils. Place in a shaker container and shake onto the carpet whenever it smells stale. Vacuum up carefully as the powder can leak out of the vacuum bag and damage the motor of your vacuum. You may want to use a "shop vac" to vacuum up most of the powder, and then finish with your household vacuum cleaner.

Carpet Spot Wipes

¼ cup vinegar

¼ cup club soda

8 drops essential oil in lemon

Combine all the ingredients. Soak 20 heavy (microwavable) paper towels in the mixture. Squeeze out the excess and store in a zip lock bag. Use for spots and spills when needed.

"They work! If you are willing to take the time to make your own cleaners, *The Joy of Green Cleaning* is a great place to start. This collection of alternatives to commercial household cleaners are easy to make out of common household ingredients, will most likely cost you less than store bought products and can work just as well!"

Dr. Jason Marshall
Laboratory Director
Toxics Use Reduction Institute,
UMass Lowell

Ant Control Solution

1/8 cup borax

1/2 cup white table sugar

or equal parts 7/2017

Combine the ingredients and spread carefully where you have seen the ants. The sugar will attract them and they will take back the sugar and borax back to the nest. The borax breaks down the skeleton of the ant and they dehydrate. You should see results in one week or less.

Tip: You can use an old turkey baster and fill it with the powder to lay a find line around cabinets or to insert into open areas where the ants may be entering your house. Do not put the mixture outside near plantings as the borax will burn plants and prevent growth. Instead place a fine line of the mixture around the perimeter of your garage. Do not use this borax mixture where children or pets could get into it.

Ant Repellent

1 container of cinnamon sticks

1 shaker container of ground cinnamon

If you see a trail of ants, you can block them with cinnamon sticks. The ants may try to go around it but will probably get discouraged and go back to the nest. Try to find where the ants are entering your home and place ground cinnamon around the entire area. The ants won't eat it. Instead it will get stuck on their legs and they will take it back to the nest. Ants don't like the smell so they will move away.

Natural Mosquito Repellant

3 drops of the following oils:

Lemon oil

Eucalyptus oil

Citronella oil

Cinnamon oil

2 tablespoons witch hazel

2 tablespoons vodka

Combine all the ingredients and place in a small spray bottle. Shake until mixed thoroughly. Shake bottle before using. Avoid using any mosquito repellant on small children and avoid if you are pregnant. Check first with your physician.

Natural Flea and Tick Repellant

6 drops lavender oil

6 drops cedar oil

1 cup witch hazel

Combine all the ingredients and place in a spray bottle. Shake until mixed thoroughly. Shake bottle before using. This does not need to be worked into the skin. The smell will repel fleas and ticks.

Natural Flea Powder

6 drops lavender oil

6 drops cedar oil

1 cup borax

Combine all the ingredients and place into a shaker container. Shake in the container until mixed thoroughly. Sprinkle on carpets and leave on carpets overnight. Keep pets and children away from carpet while it is working. Vacuum up thoroughly.

Tip: Recycle a parmesan cheese container for this mixture. Make sure you label it clearly.

Resources and Information

Where to buy it

One of the problems with "green recipes" is that they list ingredients that are difficult to find. I've found them for you! These are places you can purchase the * "star items" in this book.

Liquid castile soap - vermontsoap.com, shopgreencleaning.com or The Back Door – 866-50clean

Soda Crystals –soap-flakes.com, shopgreencleaning.com or The Back Door – 866-50clean

Soap Flakes – soap-flakes.com, shopgreencleaning.com or The Back Door – 866-50clean

Oxygen Bleach – bi-o-kleen.com, shopgreencleaning.com, mrsmeyers.com or The Back Door – 1-866-50clean

Imus All-Purpose Cleaner- imusranchfoods.com, shopgreencleaning.com or The Back Door 1-866-50clean

Cape Cod Silver Polish – capecodpolish.ca, shopgreencleaning.com or The Back Door – 1-866-50clean

Charlie's Soap – charliesoap.com, shopgreencleaning.com or The Back Door 1-866-50clean

Essential Oils - The Back Door, shopgreencleaning.com or Vermontsoap.com

Freshwave Odor Neutralizer – fresh-wave.com, shopgreencleaning.com or The Back Door 1-866-50clean

Modern Mermaid Cleaners – The Back Door, shopgreencleaning.com 1-866-50clean

Microfiber cloths- window- all-purpose - dusting - The Back Door   1-866-50clean

Microfiber mops – hardwood and tile –Ecloth.com or The Back Door 1-866-50clean

Microfiber dusting glove – casabella.com, shopgreencleaning.com or The Back Door – 1-866-50clean

Mrs. Meyer's Products– mrsmeyers.com, shopgreencleaning.com, Whole Foods Market or The Back Door 1-866-50clean

Skoy Cloths – skoycloth.com, shopgreencleaning.com or The Back Door 1-866-50clean

Seige Products – Seigechemical.com or shopgreencleaning.com

Sparkle Sponges – casabella.com, shopgreencleaning.com or The Back Door 1-866-50clean

The Cleaning Coach's Recommended Reading

Yankee Magazine's: Vinegar, Duct Tape, Milk Jugs & More
By Earl Proulx

Clean Naturally: recipes for body, home and spirit
By Sandy Maine

The Naturally Clean Home
By Karyn Siegel-Maier

How Clean Is Your House: Hundreds of handy tips to make your home sparkle.
By Kim Woodburn and Aggie MacKenzie

The Queen of Clean's Compete Cleaning Guide
By Linda Cobb

Homekeeping Handbook
By Martha Stewart

TheGreenGuide.com: A resource for consuming wisely

The Daily Green www.dailygreen.com a great web source for all things green.

Green Lighting
By Brian Clark Howard

Questions?

Call us at our green cleaning hotline at

1-508-234-4626

We will send you our our latest catalog filled with the best green cleaning products in the world. We carry the very best vacuums, cleaning tools and a full line of green cleaning products.

Visit our websites: greencleaningcoach.com

shopgreencleaning.com

Do you have a favorite great green recipe...

tip, idea or just a memory you would like to see featured in our next book? Visit my web site at greencleaningcoach.com and email me to submit your favorite green cleaning recipe or tip.

The Cleaning Coach

Cleaningcoach@yahoo.com

Don't forget to include your name, street address, phone number and e-mail address. If we select your entry, your name will appear with your submission... and you will receive a FREE copy of the book!

Notice: The information in this book has been carefully researched and all efforts have been made to ensure accuracy. Leslie Reichert and The Back Door assume no responsibility for damages or losses incurred during or as a result of following this information. All information should be studied and clearly understood before taking any action based on the information or advice in this book.

Who is Leslie Reichert, The Cleaning Coach?

Leslie Reichert is a "green" cleaning coach and the owner of the Back Door—a vacuum and homekeeping store now celebrating 20 years in business. It operates in Uxbridge, Massachusetts and nationally online at shopgreencleaning.com.

For years Leslie owned the largest residential cleaning service in the Blackstone Valley, MA. She saw, first hand, what harsh chemicals could do to your body--and she learned there are green alternatives that will work to clean your home.

Leslie has also seen scores of parents who fight a daily battle with asthma and allergies, which many believe are caused by using harsh chemicals in the home. Six years ago she realized her mission and started to share her knowledge and now encourages people in the "art" of homekeeping and green cleaning. Leslie is now a coach, presenter, and speaker for the green cleaning industry. She speaks to groups large and small, works as an advisor with companies like Martha Stewart Living Radio and presents at events such as the Chicago International Home and Housewares Show.

THREE GOOD REASONS TO GREEN YOUR CLEANING

For yourself- You must protect your body from chemicals it is simply not designed to process. There may be a correlation to the severe increase in cancers in the waste processing areas of our bodies and the chemicals we use in our homes.

For your family- We need to remember that the chemicals we use in the home stay in the home—and affect our family's indoor air quality. Our energy efficient homes not only hold in our heat, but also the chemicals that we are using for cleaning. The fumes from our cleaners can linger in our air for months. And our cleaners can affect our pets as well. Veterinarians tell us that chemicals we use on our floors can actually go through the pads of our dogs and cats feet, enter their blood stream which can damage their liver and kidneys.

For the Earth- By using green cleaning products, you help the waterways, improve air quality and find sustainable alternatives to Petro-based chemicals which are made from a non-renewable source.

If you would like more information you can follow Leslie on Facebook at http://www.facebook.com/greencleaningcoach or contact Leslie directly at cleaningcoach@yahoo.com. You can also sign up for free cleaning tips at greencleaningcoach.com.

Common Hazardous Ingredients in Cleaning Products

From http://www.lesstoxicguide.ca

Acetone- A neurotoxin, acetone may cause liver and kidney damage, and damage to the developing fetus. It is a skin and eye irritant. Found I spot treatment cleaner, mark and scuff removers and other products.

Aerosol products- Aerosol propellants may contain propane, formaldehyde, a carcinogen, neurotoxin and central nervous system depressant, methylene chloride, a carcinogen, neurotoxin and reproductive toxin, and nitrous oxide. Products applied with aerosol sprays are broken in minute particles, which can be more deeply inhaled than larger particles, which may increase their toxic effect.

Ammonia- Undiluted, ammonia is a severe eye and respiratory irritant that can cause severe burning pain, and corrosive damage including burns, cataracts and corneal damage. It can cause kidney and liver damage. Repeated or prolonged exposure to vapors can results in bronchitis and pneumonia. Found in a wide range of cleaning products. Ammonia will react with bleach to form poisonous chlorine gas that can cause burning and watering of eyes, as well as burning of the nose and mouth.

Bleach- See sodium hypochlorite

Diethanolamine (DEA)- Listed as a suspected carcinogen by the state of California, this chemical is a skin and respiratory toxicant and sever eye irritant. Used in a wide range of household cleaning products.

D-limonene- This chemical is produced by cold-pressing orange peels, the extracted oil is 90% d-limonene. It is a sensitizer, a neurotoxin, a moderate eye and skin irritant, and can trigger respiratory distress when vapors are inhaled by sensitive individuals. There is some evidence of carcinogencity. D-limonene is the active ingredient in some insecticides. It is used as a solvent in many all-purpose cleaning products, especially 'citrus' and 'orange' cleaners. Also listed on labels as citrus and orange oil.

Ethoxylated nonyl phenol: Nonyl phenols are hormone disruptors and some contain traces of ethylene oxide, a known human carcinogen. They are eye and skin irritants. Used in laundry detergents and other cleaning products.

Formaldehyde- In lab tests, formaldehyde has caused cancer and damaged DNA. Formaldehyde is also a sensitizer, with the potential to cause asthma. Several laboratory studies have shown it to be central nervous system depressant. Exposure to formaldehyde may cause joint pain, depression, headaches, chest pains, ear infections, chronic fatigue, dizziness and loss of sleep. While formaldehyde naturally occurs in the human body in minute amounts, it is estimated that 20% of people exposed to it will experience an allergic reaction. Used in a wide range of products, including some furniture polishes, formaldehyde may be released by other chemicals.

Fragrance- Fragrance on a label can indicate the presence of up to 4,000 separate ingredients, most of which are synthetic. Many compounds in fragrance are human toxins and suspected or proven carcinogens. In 1989, the US National Institute of Occupational Safety and Health evaluated 2,983 fragrance chemicals for health effects. They identified 884 of them as toxic substances. Synthetic fragrances are known to trigger asthma attacks. The US Environmental Protection Agency found that 100% of perfumes contain toluene, which can cause liver, kidney and brain damage as well as damage to a developing fetus. Symptoms reported to the FDA from fragrance exposure have included headaches, dizziness, rashes, skin discoloration, violent coughing and vomiting, and allergic skin irritation. Clinical observations by medical doctors have shown that exposure to fragrances can affect the central nervous system, causing depression, hyperactivity, irritability, inability to cope, and other behavior changes. Fragrance is a common skin irritant.

Methylene chloride- Methylene chloride is a carcinogen, a neurotoxin and a reproductive toxin. On inhalation, it can cause liver and brain damage, irregular heartbeat and even heart attack. It is a severe skin and moderate eye irritant, it is found primarily in stain removers.

Monoethanolamine- This chemical may cause liver, kidney, and reproductive damage, as well as depression of the central nervous system. Inhalation of high concentrations – when cleaning an oven for example – can cause dizziness or even coma. The chemical can also be absorbed through the skin. It is a moderate skin irritant, and a sever eye irritant. Found in many cleaning products, including oven cleaners, tub and tile cleaners, laundry pre-soaks, floor striper and carpet cleaners.

Morpholine- This corrosive ingredient can severely irritate and burn skin and eyes, and can even cause blindness if splashed in eyes. It can cause liver and kidney damage, and long-term exposure can result in bronchitis. It reacts with nitrites (added as a preservative in some products, or present as a contaminant) to form carcinogenic nitrosomines. Morphline is moderate to severe eye, skin and mucous membrane irritant. Used as a solvent in a number of cleaning products, including some furniture polishes and abrasive cleansers.

Naphthalene- This registered pesticide is listed as a suspected carcinogen in California and is most commonly found in mothballs, and some other pest repellants, as well as in deodorizers. As a reproductive toxin, it is transported across the placenta and can cause blood damage. It can cause liver and kidney damage, and corneal damage and cataracts. Skin exposure is especially dangerous to newborns.

Parabens- Parabens are hormone disruptors. Widely used in cleaning products as preservatives, paraben is usually preceded by the prefixes methyl-, ethyl-, butyl-, or propyl. Parabens may cause contact dermatitis in some individuals.

Paradichlorobenzene – This highly volatile registered pesticide is in the same chemical class as DDT. It is a suspected carcinogen, and may cause lung, liver and kidney damage. It is used in mothballs and some washroom deodorizers and urinal blocks.

Phosphoric acid- Extremely corrosive, it can severely irritate and burn the skin and eyes. Breathing vapors can make the lungs ache, and it may be toxic to the central nervous system. Fund in some liquid dishwasher detergents, metal polishes, and some disinfectants, and bathroom cleaners, especially those that remove lime and mildew.

Sodium dichloroisocyanurate dihydrate- This corrosive chemical is a severe eye, skin and respiratory irritant. It may cause liver and gastrointestinal damage, and may be toxic to the central nervous system It will react with bleach to form poisonous chloride gas that can cause burning and watering of eyes, as well as burning of the nose and mouth. It is found in some toilet bowl cleaners and deodorizers, as well as industrial detergents and some institutional dishwashing detergents.

Sodium hypochlorite (bleach) – A corrosive chemical, sodium hypochlorite is an eye, skin and respiratory irritant, as well as a sensitizer. It is especially hazardous to people with heart conditions or asthma, and can be fatal if swallowed. It may be a neurotoxin and toxic to the liver. Found in a wide range of household cleaners.

Sodium Lauryl Sulfate- Sodium lauryl sulfate (SLS) is used as a lathering agent. This chemical is a known skin irritant. It also enhances the allergic response to other toxins and allergens. The U.S government has warned manufacturers of unacceptable levels of dioxin formation in some products containing this ingredient. SLS can react with other ingredients to form cancer-causing nitrosamines.

Toulene- Exposure to toluene may cause liver, kidney and brain damage. It is also a reproductive toxin which can damage a developing fetus.

Turpentine- This chemical can cause allergic sensitization, kidney, bladder and central nervous damage. Turpentine is an eye irritant, it is found in specialty solvent cleaners, furniture polish and shoe products.

Xylene- Xylene has significant neurotoxic effects, including loss of memory. High exposure can lead to loss of consciousness and even death. Xylene has been known to cause damage to the liver, kidney and to the developing fetus. It is a severe eye and moderate skin irritant. Used in some spot removers, floor polishes, ironing aids and other products.

 # Great Green Ideas

Made in the USA
Middletown, DE
18 May 2016